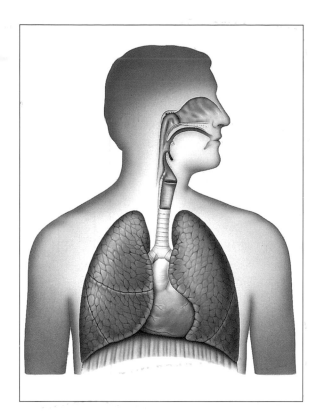

The Human Body

The Lungs and Respiratory System

Steve Parker

RSVP

RAINTREE STECK-VAUGHN
P U B L I S H E R S
The Steck-Vaughn Company

Austin, Texas

TITLES IN THE SERIES

The Heart and Circulatory System
The Stomach and Digestive System
The Brain and Nervous System
The Lungs and Respiratory System
The Skeleton and Muscular System
The Reproductive System

Published by Raintree Steck-Vaughn Publishers,
an imprint of Steck-Vaughn Company

Library of Congress Cataloging-in-Publication Data
Parker, Steve.
The lungs and respiratory system / Steve Parker.
p.   cm.—(The human body)
Includes bibliographical references and index.
Summary: Examines the different parts and functions
of the lungs and respiratory system.
ISBN 0-8172-4803-X
1. Respiratory organs—Juvenile literature.
2. Lungs—Juvenile literature.
3. Respiration—Juvenile literature.
[1. Lungs. 2. Respiratory system. 3. Respiration.]
I. Title. II. Series: Parker, Steve. Human Body.
QP121.P274   1997
612.2—dc21   96-43516

Printed in Italy. Bound in the United States.
1 2 3 4 5 6 7 8 9 0 01 00 99 98 97

Picture Acknowledgments
The publishers would like to thank the following for use of their photographs:
Impact 45; Science Photo Library 4, 11, 15, 17, 20, 25, 35;
Zefa 26, 36, 37, 39; Wayland Picture Library 29.

CONTENTS

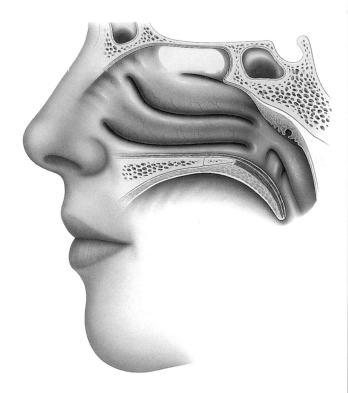

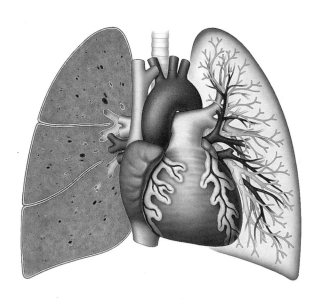

Introduction

Every few seconds, every day, throughout life, the body breathes. It takes some air into its lungs and then pushes the air out again. The movements of breathing are called bodily respiration. Many other animals breathe in the same way as humans, including cats, dogs, and other mammals, and birds and frogs. Breathing is a sign of life. If we stop breathing for more than a few minutes, life ebbs away and the body begins to die.

Why do we breathe? The answer has to do with body chemistry. The human body, like all living things, needs energy for life. This energy powers the many **biochemical** processes and reactions that happen inside the body, every second. The energy comes from food, which is broken down and absorbed into the body by the digestive system.

Digested food contains energy in a chemical form. To release this energy, the digested food must undergo a series of chemical changes. These are called cellular **respiration**. They happen in the billions of microscopic cells that make up the body. During these changes, the food is combined with oxygen. Oxygen is the gas that makes up one-fifth of the air around us. It is the job of the lungs and respiratory system to get this oxygen from the air. The respiratory system also removes a by-product of cellular respiration, carbon dioxide. This would be poisonous if it were allowed to build up inside the body.

So there are two kinds of respiration. One is cellular respiration, the series of chemical changes inside a cell. These chemical changes release energy from food, and they require oxygen and produce carbon dioxide. The other kind of respiration is bodily respiration, the movements of breathing, also called ventilation.

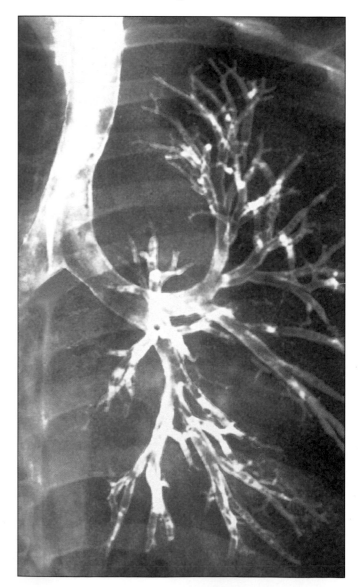

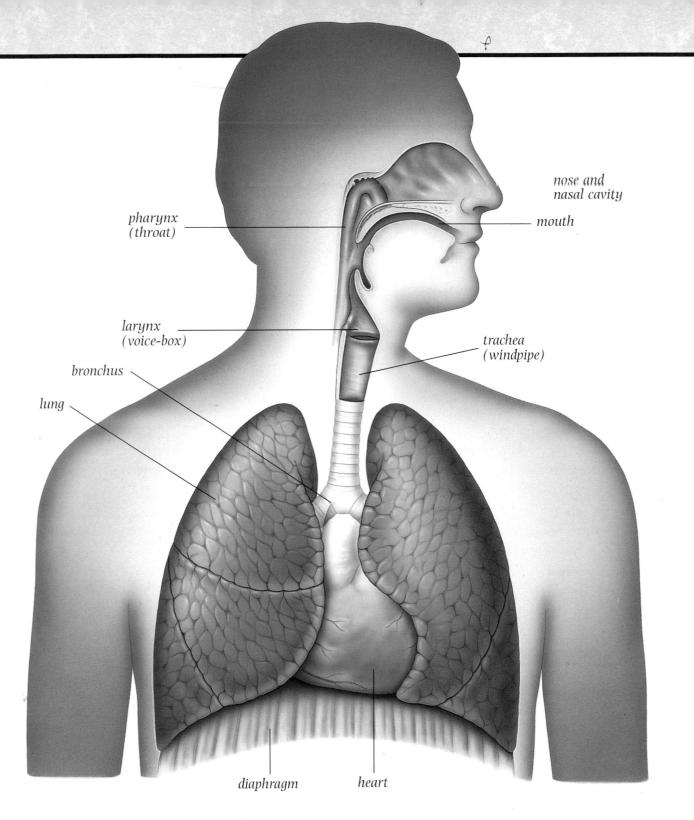

nose and nasal cavity

pharynx (throat)

mouth

larynx (voice-box)

trachea (windpipe)

bronchus

lung

diaphragm

heart

◄ **This type of X-ray picture, called a bronchogram, shows the main air tubes or airways in the lungs, inside the chest. It can help doctors see the structure of the larger airways and so recognize any defects.**

▲

A body system consists of body parts that work together to carry out a particular important task. The task of the respiratory system is to obtain oxygen from the air and pass it to the blood, which carries the oxygen all around the body. The main parts of the respiratory system are in the head, neck, and chest.

The Nose

You can breathe in and out through your nose or mouth (or both). But the nose is usually the main entrance for air going into the respiratory system. It is the nose's job to make the incoming air warm, moist, and clean, so that the air will be suitable to flow down into the lungs.

The framework of·the nose is made of curved plates of **cartilage** (gristle). These plates hold open the two entrance holes, called the nostrils, or external nares. Inside the nose is an air chamber, the nasal cavity. It is divided down the middle by one of the cartilage plates, called the septal cartilage. Each half of the nasal cavity is about the size of the three main fingers on one hand.

The roof, sides, and floor of the nasal cavity are formed by the skull bones. The nostrils open into the lower front of the cavity, and an opening at the lower rear of the cavity leads down past the rear of the mouth, into the **pharynx**, or throat. During breathing, air flows in and out through the nasal cavity, mainly along its floor.

The inner lining of the nasal cavity is called the nasal mucosa. It is soft and moist, and a lot of blood flows through it, making it red and warm. The nasal mucosa continually makes thin, watery, slimy **mucus** to cover itself. The mucus helps to protect the mucosa and keep it from drying out in the constant flow of air. It also moistens the air going past to the lungs,

The nasal cavity is the large air chamber inside the nose. It has various openings, including the nostrils to the outside, the nasopharyngeal opening to the throat, and passages to the sinus air chambers set into the skull bone. ▶

and the many blood vessels in the lining warm the air, too. Also the sticky mucus, along with hairs near the nostrils, filter the air by trapping floating particles. The mucus gradually passes down into the throat where it is naturally swallowed. If the mucus is too plentiful, such as during a cold or hay fever, it can be blown out through the nostrils.

A human skull has a hole where the nose should be. That is because the projecting part of the nose is made not from bone, but from plates of cartilage. These soon rot away after death, so they leave a hole.

The main cartilage is the septal cartilage, which divides the nasal cavity into two halves. The cartilages on the upper sides of the nose are the lateral nasal cartilages. On the lower side, above the nostril, is the major alar cartilage. Behind this are three or four smaller, minor alar cartilages.

The nose cartilages are more flexible than bone. They can bend considerably before they break. But a blow on the nose can crack cartilages, even though it does not break bone.

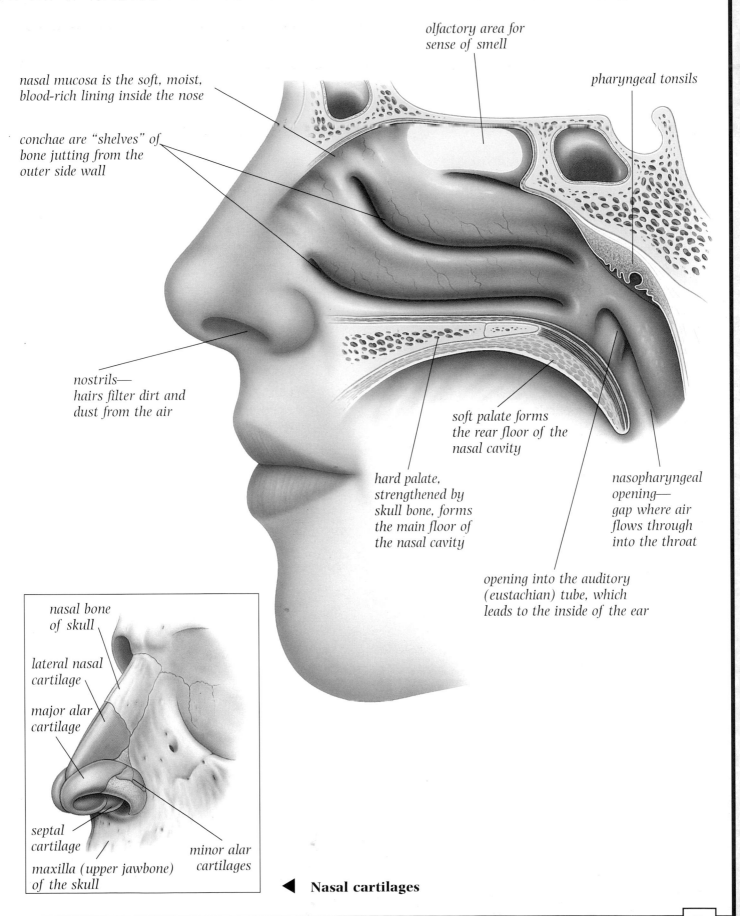

olfactory area for
sense of smell

nasal mucosa is the soft, moist,
blood-rich lining inside the nose

pharyngeal tonsils

conchae are "shelves" of
bone jutting from the
outer side wall

nostrils—
hairs filter dirt and
dust from the air

soft palate forms
the rear floor of the
nasal cavity

hard palate,
strengthened by
skull bone, forms
the main floor of
the nasal cavity

nasopharyngeal
opening—
gap where air
flows through
into the throat

opening into the auditory
(eustachian) tube, which
leads to the inside of the ear

nasal bone
of skull

lateral nasal
cartilage

major alar
cartilage

septal
cartilage

maxilla (upper jawbone)
of the skull

minor alar
cartilages

◀ **Nasal cartilages**

Sense of Smell

How many scents and odors have you smelled today? You have probably experienced many smells, some of them without realizing it. They might include scented soap, flavored toothpaste, milk, orange juice, breakfast foods, flowers, and vehicle fumes.

The sense of smell is very important to the body's survival. It helps to check foods and drinks, to make sure they are not bad, rotten, or spoiled. This is less important today because most foods are sold in a safe condition, but in Stone Age times people had to gather, hunt, and scavenge their own meals.

Smells also alert us to dangers, such as the smoke from a fire. We also use smells to give pleasure and enjoyment, such as the scent of perfume and flowers, and the aroma of delicious food.

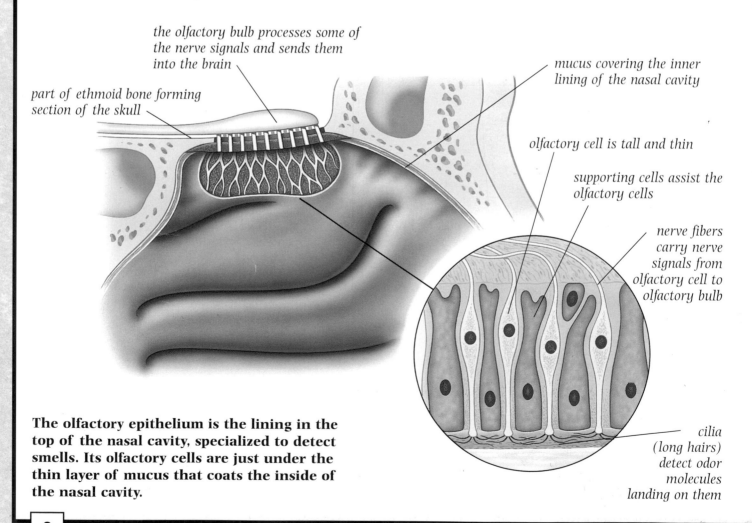

the olfactory bulb processes some of the nerve signals and sends them into the brain

part of ethmoid bone forming section of the skull

mucus covering the inner lining of the nasal cavity

olfactory cell is tall and thin

supporting cells assist the olfactory cells

nerve fibers carry nerve signals from olfactory cell to olfactory bulb

cilia (long hairs) detect odor molecules landing on them

The olfactory epithelium is the lining in the top of the nasal cavity, specialized to detect smells. Its olfactory cells are just under the thin layer of mucus that coats the inside of the nasal cavity.

Smells are tiny odor molecules or particles drifting in the air. The parts that detect them are two patches of lining in the roof of the nasal cavity. They are called olfactory epithelia ("olfactory" means having to do with smell). Each is only the area of a thumbnail, yet they contain millions of tiny olfactory cells. Each of these has up to 20 long hairs, called **cilia**, which stick into the mucus layer on the inside of the nasal cavity. When certain odor molecules touch the cilia, they make the olfactory receptor cells generate nerve signals. The signals pass along nerves to the brain, for sorting and identification.

Breathed-in air contains many different smells. The brain only pays attention to important smells or to changes in the strength of a smell. You notice a new smell, but then it seems to fade quickly. However, it is probably still there. When another person arrives, he or she smells it at once. This "fading" of the sense of smell, even when the smell is still there, is called habituation. It also happens with the body's other senses, especially taste and touch.

When you want to get the smell of something, you take a good sniff. Normally, air flows through the nasal cavity along its bottom part. A sniff makes the air currents swirl into the upper part of the nasal cavity. This brings more of the odor substances in the air into contact with the olfactory epithelium, where they can be detected.

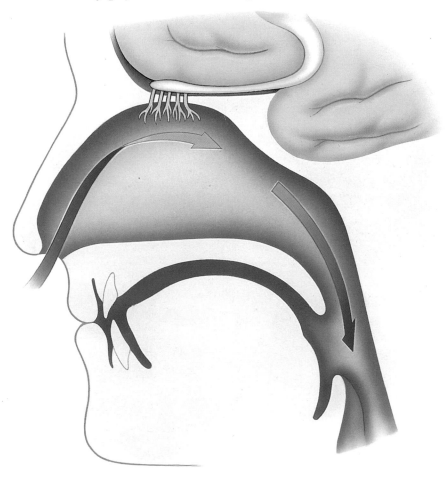

▲ **Air currents flowing up to the olfactory area**

FACT BOX

Each of the two patches of olfactory epithelium has about 10 million olfactory cells.

These cells live for only a month, then they die and are replaced.

An average person can detect and tell apart about 10,000 smells.

Some smells can be sensed at very low levels or concentrations—only one part of smell in 30 billion parts of air. One example is the stink of a skunk.

The Sinuses

When you speak, air passes through your mouth—and also through your nose. Try talking while holding your nose, to see what happens. The air flowing out through the nose helps to give more sound quality and feature to the voice. This is partly because the nasal cavity is not the only air space inside the upper head. There are eight more air chambers, called paranasal sinuses, or more usually, **sinuses**.

The sinuses are "holes" set into the skull bones. There are four pairs of sinuses, and they are named after the skull bones that house them, the ethmoidal, frontal, sphenoidal, and maxillary sinuses. The ethmoidal sinuses are not air-filled cavities or caves like the other sinuses. They are more like sponges or honeycombs of many tiny air holes.

▼ **The skull is made up of many curved bones, fixed firmly together. The four pairs of sinuses are inside the thicknesses of some of these bones. The largest are the maxillary sinuses.**

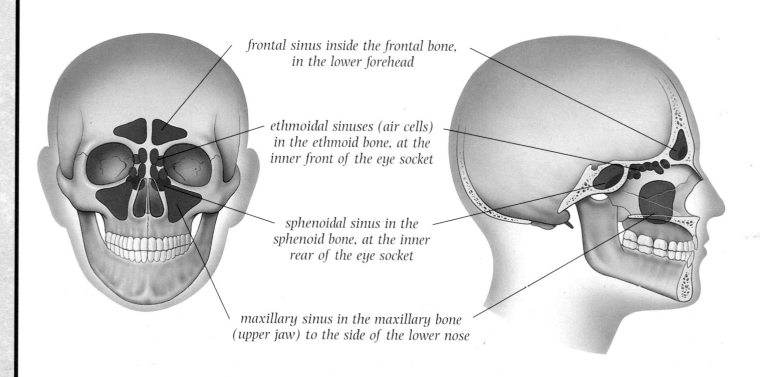

frontal sinus inside the frontal bone, in the lower forehead

ethmoidal sinuses (air cells) in the ethmoid bone, at the inner front of the eye socket

sphenoidal sinus in the sphenoid bone, at the inner rear of the eye socket

maxillary sinus in the maxillary bone (upper jaw) to the side of the lower nose

The sinuses are connected to the main nasal cavity by holes and air passages. The nasal mucosa of the nasal cavity extends through these holes and air passages and also forms the lining of the sinuses. When a cold affects the nose, making its lining swollen and sore, this swelling may extend into the sinuses. The condition is then called sinusitis, and it can be very painful. If it affects the frontal sinuses, there is pain in the lower part of the frontal bone of the forehead, just above the eyes.

The sinuses help to make the skull and head lighter. They contain air, rather than heavy bone. The sinuses also affect the sounds of speech. They work like amplifying and resonating chambers to give the voice more character and "color." When a person has a cold and the nasal cavity and sinuses are blocked with extra mucus, the voice seems featureless and "flat."

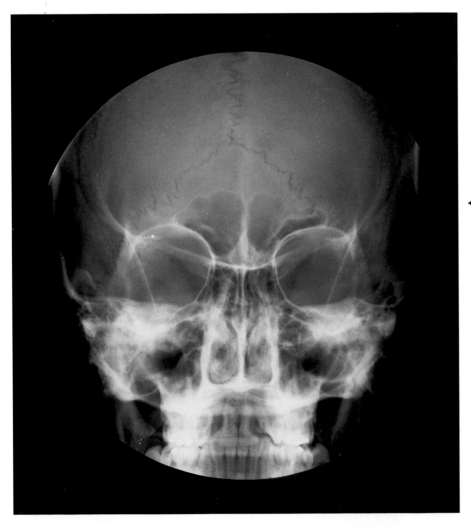

◄ In this X ray of the skull, the sinuses are the dark areas. Sometimes the sinuses become repeatedly infected and blocked by swelling and mucus. This causes discomfort and pain. A modern paranasal endoscope is a very thin tube that can be bent and steered into the main sinuses through the nose. A doctor can look through the endoscope to see the problem, take samples, and give treatment by unblocking and washing out the sinus chambers.

The Throat

After the nose and nasal cavity, the next passage for air going down to the lungs is the pharynx. This is divided into two parts. The upper part is the nasopharynx. It is behind the soft palate, the bent-down rear part of the floor of the nasal cavity. The lower part is the oropharynx or throat, which is a continuation from the back of the mouth.

The oropharynx is also the second part of the passageway for food and drink after the mouth, so it is a dual passage for both the respiratory and digestive systems. The pharynx has a smooth, moist, tough covering.

This covering must cope with the drying effects of air when breathing and the rubbing effects of food as it is swallowed.

Below the pharynx is the **larynx**, usually called the voice box. This is the inlet for air flowing down into the lower respiratory system. Swallowed food passes through the throat and down behind the larynx, into the gullet, or esophagus. During swallowing, muscular movements pull the larynx out of the way, and a flap called the epiglottis moves to cover it. This prevents food from entering the larynx, which could cause choking.

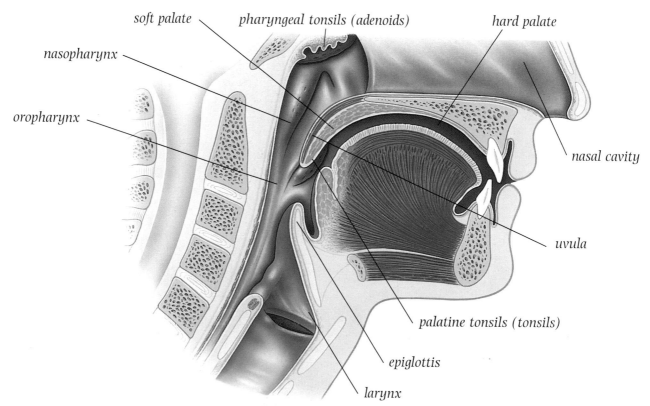

soft palate · pharyngeal tonsils (adenoids) · hard palate · nasopharynx · oropharynx · nasal cavity · uvula · palatine tonsils (tonsils) · epiglottis · larynx

▲ **This diagram shows the structures of the pharynx and larynx.**

The pharynx has a ring of defenses against infection, made up of the adenoids high up at the back of the nose and the tonsils lower down at the sides of the throat. These structures are similar to lymph glands and protect the entrance to the inside of the chest by fighting invading germs and by swelling during infection.

After food has been chewed, a small portion, called a bolus, is separated off by the tongue, and pushed to the back of the mouth. As it enters and touches the walls of the oropharynx, it triggers the swallowing reflex.

This is an automatic sequence of muscle contractions in the rear mouth, the oropharynx, and the upper gullet (esophagus), to ensure that swallowed food passes safely into the gullet.

These diagrams show the processes of swallowing a bolus of food. If we try to eat and talk at the same time, the top of the larynx stays open and unprotected, and food may get on top of it. If so, this causes us to cough and, in serious cases, to choke. When this happens, we say that the food has "gone down the wrong way."

▼

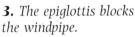
1. The bolus of food is pushed to the back of the mouth.

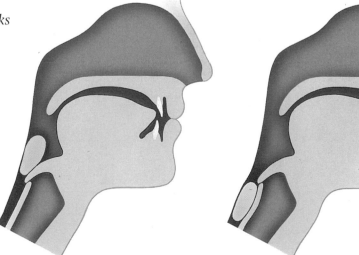
2. The soft palate blocks the nasal cavity.

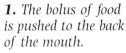
3. The epiglottis blocks the windpipe.

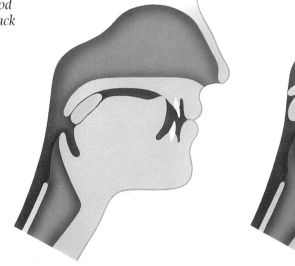
4. The bolus of food is pushed into the esophagus.

The Larynx

The respiratory system's main job is to get oxygen from the air into the body's blood. But the air flowing through the system has a very useful side effect. It shakes or rattles two thin shelves of tough, skinlike substance called the vocal cords, inside the larynx or voice box. These vibrate, or move back and forth very fast, in the airstream. As they vibrate, they make a noise.

The noise from the vocal cords is the sound of the human voice. We use it to speak. This secondary use of the respiratory system allows us to communicate our thoughts, ideas, and feelings to each other. We also use our vocal cords to make many other sounds, such as laughter, sobs, screams, and hums. These sounds also communicate our feelings and emotions. Speech and other sounds from the vocal cords are together known as vocalizations.

The larynx has a framework of nine stiff, curved plates of cartilage. The largest is the thyroid cartilage, which can be seen under the skin of the neck as the "Adam's apple." Just above the true vocal cords are similar parts called false vocal cords. These do not make any sounds.

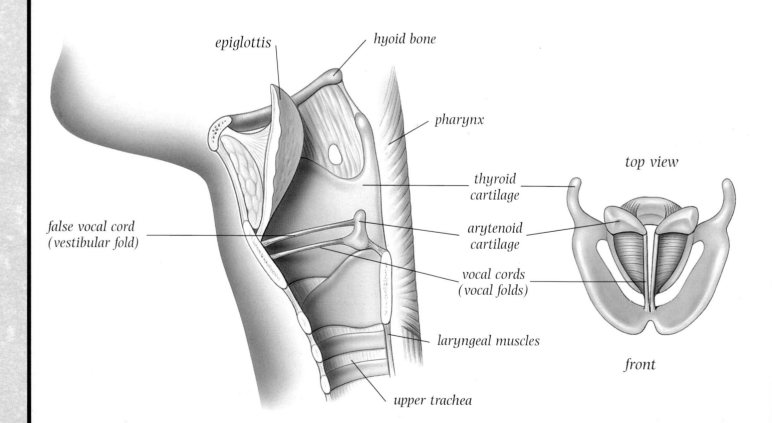

epiglottis

hyoid bone

pharynx

top view

thyroid cartilage

arytenoid cartilage

false vocal cord (vestibular fold)

vocal cords (vocal folds)

laryngeal muscles

front

upper trachea

The vocal cords work mainly when the body breathes out, and air flows up from the lungs and windpipe. Talking while breathing in is much more difficult. The cords are not like the freely vibrating strings on a guitar or violin. They are flaps or "shelves" that stick out from the sides of the larynx. They are also known as the vocal folds, which gives a better description of their structure.

The cords are apart for normal breathing. To make a sound, they move together, so that the gap between them is very narrow. They are also stretched slightly. These movements are made by several sets of muscles in the neck, which alter the position of the thyroid and arytenoid cartilages. The vocal cords are anchored to these stiff cartilages and are pulled when the cartilages move. The cords are stretched longer and tighter for higher-pitched sounds and become shorter and floppier for low, deep sounds. The vocal cords are usually longer and thicker in men, which is why men's voices are deeper than women's.

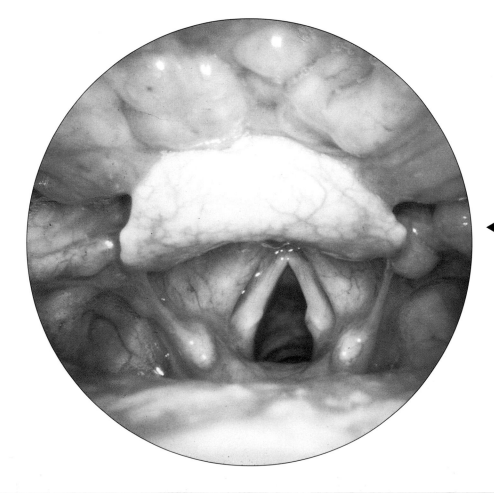

◄ A laryngoscope is a medical instrument for looking down the throat into the larynx. Through a laryngoscope, a doctor can see the inside of the larynx and the vocal cords. Here, the cords are apart for normal, quiet breathing, leaving a triangular gap between them called the glottis. Muscles tilt and swivel them together for speech, so the gap is reduced to a narrow slit.

The Trachea

On its journey into the respiratory system, air comes in through the nose or mouth and then passes through the pharynx and larynx. The next part of the air passage, or respiratory airway, is the **trachea**, or windpipe. The parts of the system, called the upper respiratory tract, are above the larynx. This tract includes the nasal cavity and pharynx down to the larynx. The lower respiratory tract consists of the trachea itself, the branching air tubes at its lower end, and the lungs.

The trachea extends from the larynx, which is really its uppermost part, down through the lower neck and between the shoulders, to the upper chest. Directly behind it is the esophagus, carrying swallowed food down to the stomach. The trachea branches at its lower end into two large air tubes called **bronchi**.

In an average adult, the trachea is about 4 in. (10–11 cm) long and 0.5 to 0.75 in. (1.5–2 cm) wide. In a newborn, it is very narrow—about the size of the inside of a ballpoint pen. The trachea is kept open by C-shaped rings of cartilage. There are between sixteen and twenty rings of cartilage, regularly spaced along its length. Some rings branch into two parts around the sides. The open parts of the C-shaped rings are at the back, next to the esophagus.

The rings of cartilage allow the trachea to bend with movements of the neck and chest. They also keep the trachea open against internal body pressure, allowing air to pass up and down to and from the lungs.

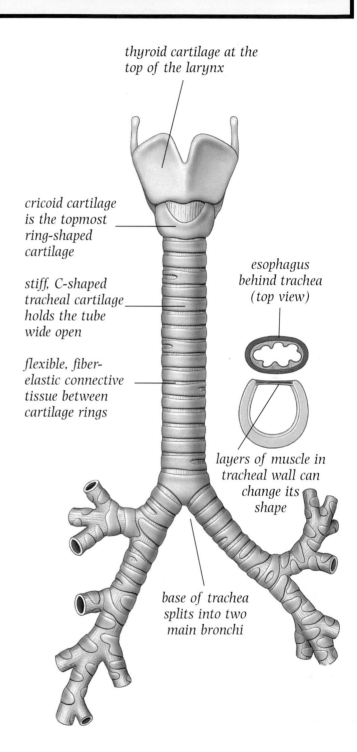

thyroid cartilage at the top of the larynx

cricoid cartilage is the topmost ring-shaped cartilage

stiff, C-shaped tracheal cartilage holds the tube wide open

flexible, fiber-elastic connective tissue between cartilage rings

esophagus behind trachea (top view)

layers of muscle in tracheal wall can change its shape

base of trachea splits into two main bronchi

Many parts of the respiratory system, including the trachea, have a lining bearing thousands of microscopic hairs, called cilia. The cilia wave or beat back and forth with a rowing motion. This moves the layer of mucus covering them, which lines the system. The mucus is produced continuously. It traps dust, dirt, and other particles, and it is then pushed along by the cilia like a moving, sticky carpet. In the trachea and lower airways, the cilia push the mucus upward to the throat. There it is swallowed into the esophagus. We may give a small cough to help the mucus out of the trachea and larynx, into the esophagus. This is called "clearing the throat." The whole process helps to keep the airways clear.

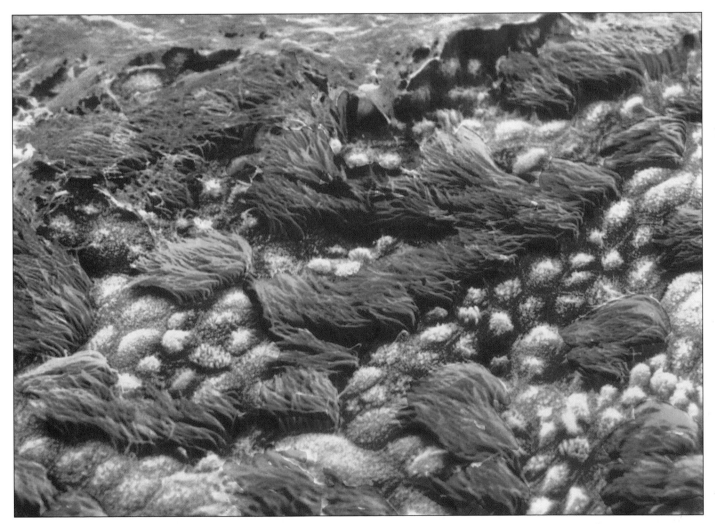

◄ **The trachea has muscles in its wall. These can make it longer and narrower, or shorter and wider, to cope with the movements of breathing and other body movements that lengthen or shorten the neck, as when bringing the chin down to the chest.**

▲ **This picture shows cilia beating to remove dust and dirt particles.**

The Lungs

The lungs take up most of the room inside the chest. They look like shiny, smooth, pink-gray sponges. In young children they are mostly pink, and in older people they gradually turn gray, or even black. That is due to bits of dust and dirt that gradually gather in them over a lifetime. The color change and blackening is far more noticeable in people who smoke, compared with nonsmokers. It is also slightly more noticeable in people who live in the city compared with people who live in the country.

▼ **A front view of the lungs showing their main parts, or lobes, and the heart nestling between them.**

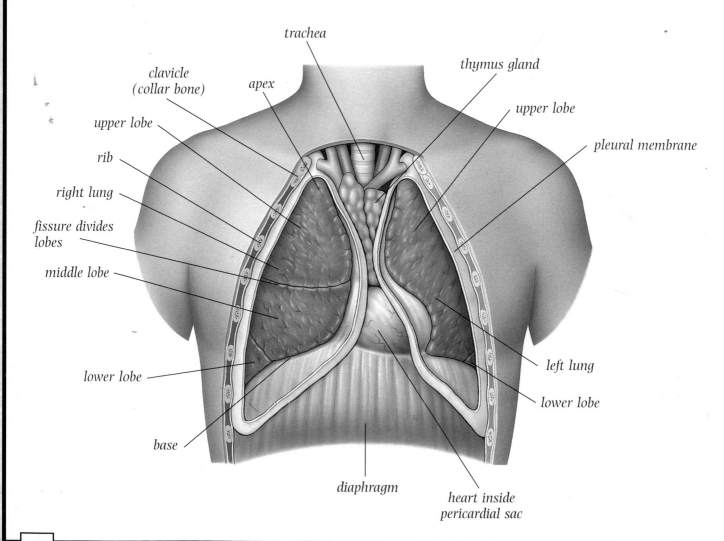

trachea

thymus gland

clavicle
(collar bone)

apex

upper lobe

upper lobe

pleural membrane

rib

right lung

fissure divides
lobes

middle lobe

lower lobe

left lung

lower lobe

base

diaphragm

heart inside
pericardial sac

Each lung is roughly cone-shaped, with a thin upper tip called the apex and a wide base. The heart and main blood vessels are between the lungs. The left lung has two main parts, or lobes, and the right lung has three lobes. The left lung is slightly smaller than the right lung, because it has a scooped-out shape where the heart sits.

▼ **Each of the pleural membranes lines one side of the thoracic cavity and folds back to cover the surface of the lung on that side. There is a very thin layer of oily liquid, pleural fluid, between the two layers of each pleural membrane. As you breathe, the chest expands and so do the lungs. But the two layers of pleural membrane stay in close contact, sliding over each other lubricated by pleural fluid.**

The upper tips of the lungs come above the shoulders and behind and above the clavicles (collar bones) in the upper chest. The bases of the lungs sit on a large domed sheet of muscle, the **diaphragm**. So the bases have a scooped-out shape in the middle, as though sitting on an upturned bowl. Each lung curves out and down around its lower edges, especially at the sides, almost down to the lowest ribs.

The soft, delicate lungs and heart tissue are well protected inside a "cage" formed by the twelve pairs of ribs, the sternum (breastbone) at the front, and the vertebral column (backbone) at the rear. The bones move where they are joined, so the cage is flexible, to allow the movements of breathing.

The lungs, heart, and main blood vessels almost entirely fill the space inside the chest, called the thoracic cavity. Each lung is covered by a slippery, shiny, thin sheet called the pleural membrane. This lubricates the movements of breathing, as shown in the diagram opposite.

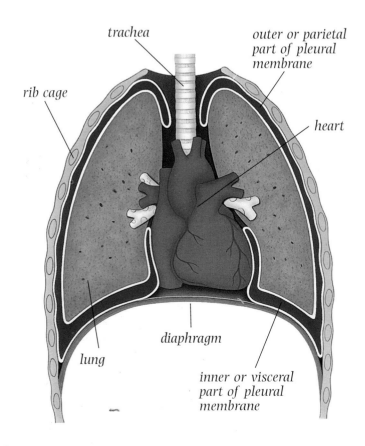

trachea

outer or parietal part of pleural membrane

rib cage

heart

diaphragm

lung

inner or visceral part of pleural membrane

FACT BOX

- When a person breathes in as much as possible, the two lungs expand to hold 6.4 qts. (6 l) of air in a man, and about 4.5 qts. (4.2 l) in a woman.

- There are about 0.2 qts. (0.2 l) of air in the nasal cavity, pharynx, larynx, trachea, and main lung airways.

- There is a teaspoonful of pleural fluid between the layers of pleural membrane around each lung.

Inside the Lungs

The lungs look very different inside, compared with their smooth, shiny exteriors. There are six parts to the inside of each lung, and these fit together in a very complicated way. First are the tiny air bubbles, or **alveoli**, where oxygen passes from the air into the blood (see page 24). Second is the supporting or interstitial tissue of the lungs, which fills the gaps between the other structures. Together, the alveoli and interstitial tissue give the lungs a spongy, elastic texture.

The other parts inside the lungs are shaped like trees with many branches. The third part is the bronchial tree—the system of air tubes or airways. It begins with the main airway or primary bronchus, which branches from the lower end of the trachea. The primary bronchus divides again into narrower airways, the secondary bronchi, and so on, until the tubes are too small to see (shown on the next page). At the end of the branches are the alveoli. The fourth part is the branching system of nerves. There are nerves in the chest, just as in other parts of the body. They pick up sensations such as pain, and they control the muscles in the walls of the airways and **arteries**.

The fifth and sixth parts are branching networks of blood vessels. One network consists of arteries, and it brings stale, **deoxygenated** blood from the heart into the lungs. It is known as the arterial pulmonary tree ("pulmonary" means having to do with the lungs). The other is the venous pulmonary tree. It takes the refreshed, **oxygenated** blood from the lungs back to the heart, to be circulated all over the body. In addition, the lungs have their own blood supply. This consists of the bronchial arteries and veins and their branches.

▲ Normal X-ray pictures show up hard, dense substances, such as bones, but they do not pick out soft tissues, such as the blood vessels and airways in the lung. This is a computed X-ray tomography scan (CT scan) of the chest of a healthy young woman showing normal lungs with the heart between them. CT and MRI scans allow interwoven sets of air tubes, blood vessels, and other structures deep in the lungs to be seen.

The interior of the lungs ▶ is a complex web of many tubes and vessels. Most of these enter or leave each lung at a place called the root, on the lung's middle-facing surface.

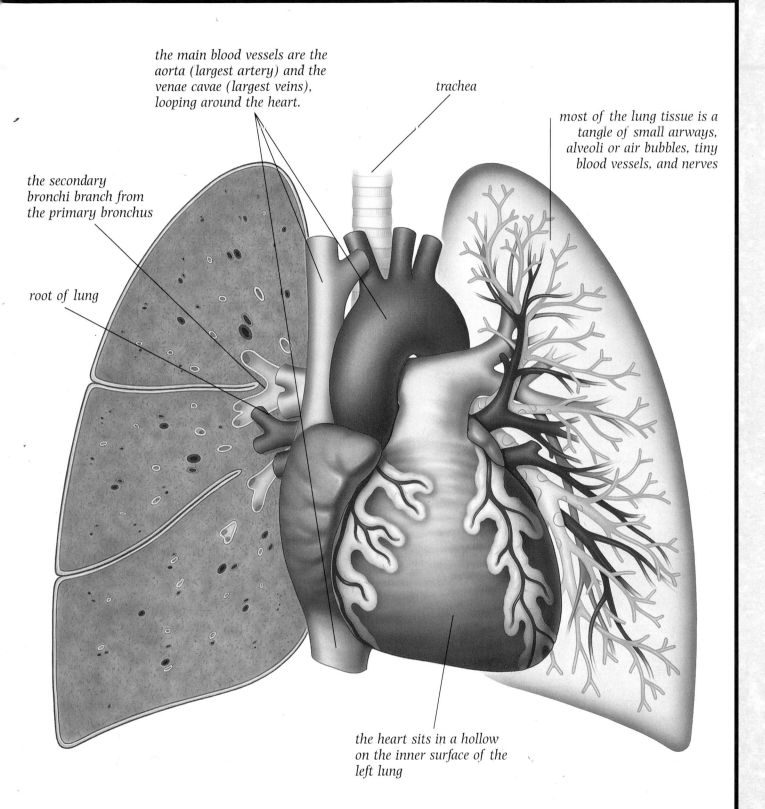

the main blood vessels are the aorta (largest artery) and the venae cavae (largest veins), looping around the heart.

trachea

most of the lung tissue is a tangle of small airways, alveoli or air bubbles, tiny blood vessels, and nerves

the secondary bronchi branch from the primary bronchus

root of lung

the heart sits in a hollow on the inner surface of the left lung

The Small Vessels and Airways

Look more closely at a lung and you can see the small parts in marvelous detail. Each of the blood-vessel trees begins with either the main artery or the main **vein** as the "trunk." This divides and branches until it forms microscopic "twigs." In the arterial tree, the smallest arteries are called **arterioles**. These divide even further into the smallest blood tubes, known as **capillaries**. In the venous tree, the smallest veins are called **venules**.

The two pulmonary trees of arteries and veins are joined at their "twigs." That is because blood flows from the smallest arteries, through the capillaries and on into the smallest veins, and then to the larger veins. But the blood-vessel trees are not joined end to end. Their trunks are side by side, and their branches are meshed together.

This applies to all the other treelike structures in the lungs. One is the bronchial tree, whose airways branch in the same way. They divide into smaller and smaller tubes, known as bronchi. The narrowest are the terminal bronchi. They may be only 0.04 in. (1 mm) wide, but they have muscles in their walls and rings of cartilage to keep them open wide, just as in the much larger trachea and bronchi.

This branching process continues into even narrower air tubes called **bronchioles**. After about fifteen sets of divisions from the original primary bronchus, the air tubes are much thinner than human hairs. They are called terminal bronchioles, and they end in alveoli.

Smaller and smaller branches of nerves, bronchial blood vessels, lymph vessels, and other body systems follow the same branching pattern, down to microscopic sizes. Between this maze of tiny tubes and vessels is the interstitial tissue of the lung, which fills the gaps and gives strength and support to the branching systems.

The smallest "twigs" of the various treelike parts of the lung are far too small to see with the unaided eye. Air tubes, blood and lymph vessels, nerves, and other structures divide many times. ▶

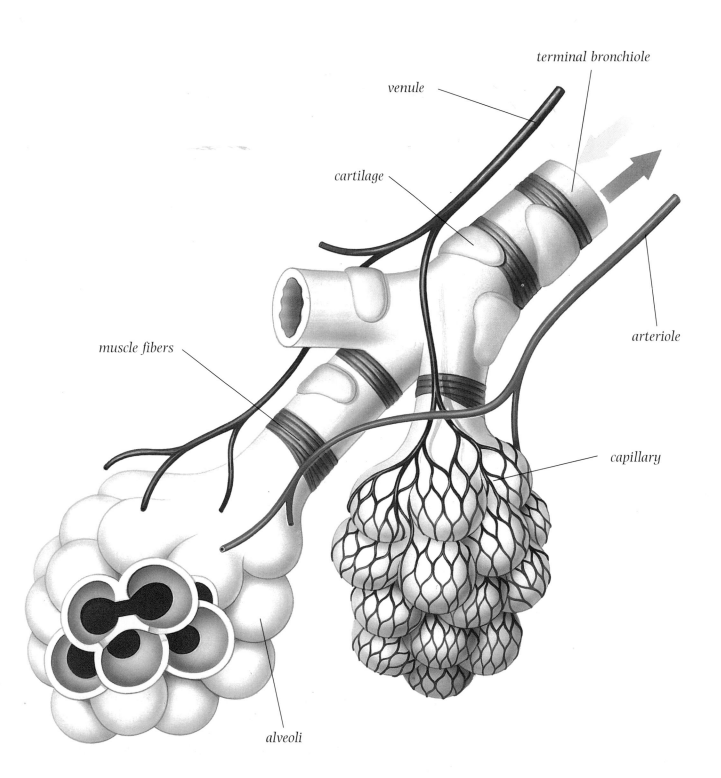

terminal bronchiole

venule

cartilage

muscle fibers

arteriole

capillary

alveoli

Alveoli

The lung's smallest airways—the tips of the twigs of the bronchial tree—are the terminal bronchioles. They end in groups of alveoli. The alveoli on a terminal bronchiole resemble a bunch of grapes hanging on a twig.

Like grapes in a mesh bag, each bunch of alveoli is surrounded by a network of the smallest blood vessels, called capillaries. These lie touching the outside of the wall of each alveolus. Blood flows through the capillaries from the smallest arterioles and on into the smallest veins.

It is estimated that there are 250 to 300 million alveoli in each lung. Flattened out, they provide a huge surface area for **gas exchange** to take place. Oxygen passes from the air into the alveoli and into the blood flowing through the capillaries around them.

In places, the walls of the alveolus and the walls of the capillary on the outside of the alveolus are only one cell thick. So the distance between the air and the blood may be less than 0.00004 in. (one micrometer). On average, it is about two to three times that distance. This is a very thin barrier for oxygen to cross. At the same time, carbon dioxide crosses it the other way, going from the blood in the capillaries to the air inside the alveoli.

▼ **This diagram shows a single alveolus. Surrounding it are the red blood cells in their capillaries, collecting oxygen and giving up waste carbon dioxide.**

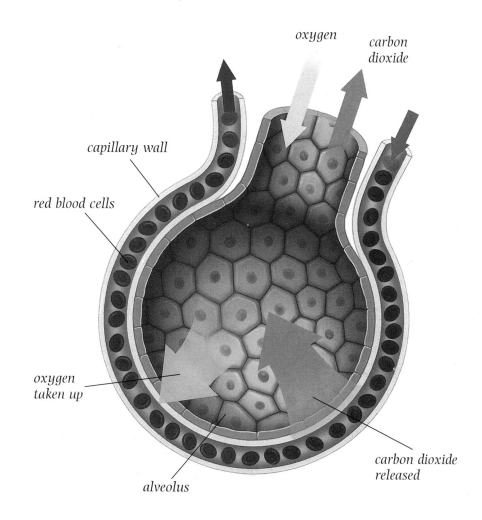

oxygen

carbon dioxide

capillary wall

red blood cells

oxygen taken up

carbon dioxide released

alveolus

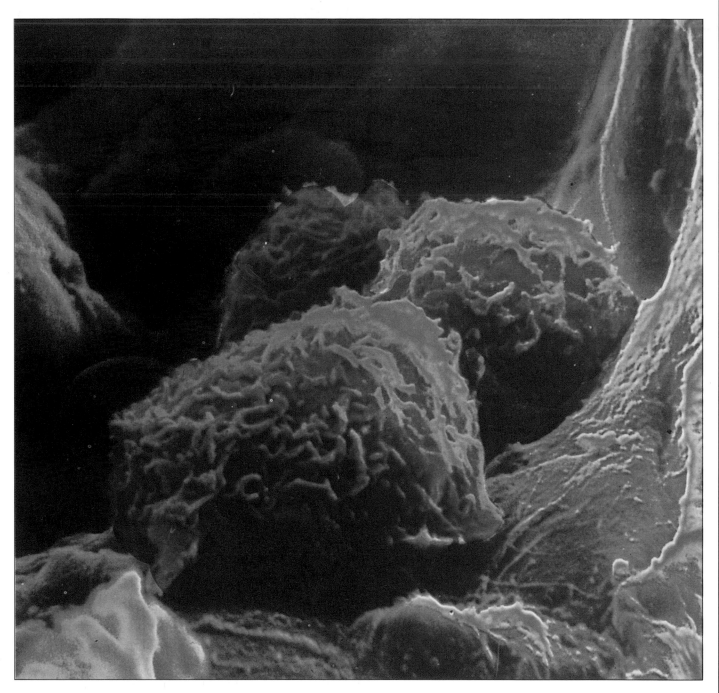

▲

The terminal bronchioles and alveoli are not lined by cilia, like those that sweep away sticky mucus and keep the trachea clean. They have a different cleaning system. This consists of microscopic cells called macrophages, which are part of the body's disease-fighting immune defense system. Macrophages can change their shape and move through the alveoli and airways. They scavenge for bits of dust, germs, and other debris, "eat" them whole, and keep the alveoli clean.

The Need for Oxygen

The respiratory system is designed to obtain oxygen from the air and pass it to the blood, which carries the oxygen around the whole body. The system also gets rid of the waste product carbon dioxide from the blood, passing it out into the air.

The need for oxygen is not unique to the human body. Apart from a few specialized types of bacteria and other **microbes**, all living things need a constant supply of oxygen to live. Oxygen is a vital part of a series of chemical changes or reactions, called cellular respiration (sometimes also called aerobic respiration).

Cellular respiration happens inside every one of the billions of cells that make up the body. Its chemical changes begin with oxygen and a high-energy substance obtained from digested food, such as the sugar glucose. It ends with the production of carbon dioxide and the release of energy from the glucose. The cell uses this energy to provide the power for thousands of other chemical processes that happen every second. So food provides the energy-rich "fuel" that keeps the body going.

This series of chemical changes is long and complicated, with more than twenty stages. But it can be simplified as a chemical summary, or equation, showing what goes in at the beginning and what comes out at the end.

▲ The human body can last for only a few minutes without oxygen. When divers go under the water, they take an oxygen supply with them. They take oxygen in scuba tanks or oxygen is pumped down a tube into the diving suit. Thin air at the tops of mountains contains little oxygen, so mountaineers also take an oxygen supply. In all these cases, it is not pure oxygen that is breathed, but oxygen mixed with other gases.

$$C_6H_{12}O_6 + 6O_2 = 6CO_2 + 6H_2O + ENERGY$$

The equation shows that one molecule of glucose plus six molecules of oxygen are changed by cellular respiration into six molecules of carbon dioxide and six molecules of water, plus energy.

The oxygen comes from the air and is taken into the body by the respiratory system.

The glucose is a type of sugar. It is obtained by digesting food and breaking it down into smaller and smaller pieces and then breaking these into smaller and smaller molecules. Foods that are rich in glucose include sugary and starchy foods, such as cookies, bread, rice, potatoes, and pasta.

Carbon dioxide is an unwanted by-product of respiration. If it was allowed to collect in body cells or in the blood, it would upset the body's internal chemistry. It needs to be continually removed from the body by the respiratory system.

The water is just ordinary water, like pure water from the tap. It seeps into all body parts. The water made by cellular respiration and other chemical processes inside cells is called "water of metabolism," and about 11 oz. (320 ml) is produced every 24 hours.

The energy is used for other chemical reactions in the cell. It is carried around the cell by a special high-energy substance called ATP (adenosine triphosphate).

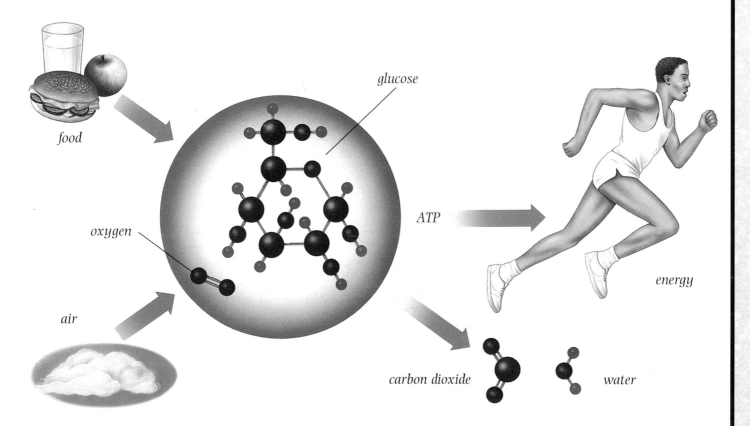

food

glucose

oxygen

air

ATP

energy

carbon dioxide

water

▲   **Glucose from food is delivered by the blood to every cell. Inside the cell it is used to make ATP, in which energy is carried.**

Movements of Breathing

The energy that cellular respiration releases from foods is used for thousands of processes in the body. One is breathing. The movements of breathing are powered by muscles. The shortening or contraction of a muscle happens as a result of chemical changes inside the muscle. Energy is needed for the chemical changes to take place.

▼ **The main muscles of breathing are the diaphragm and intercostals.**

Breathing in is called inspiration and breathing out is called expiration. Inspiration is the muscle-powered part of the breathing process, and it involves several sets of muscles. The two major muscle sets are the diaphragm and the **intercostals**. The diaphragm is the large dome-shaped muscle under the lungs, like an upturned bowl. It forms the division between the chest above and the abdomen below. The intercostals are long, straplike muscles between the ribs.

Inspiration

1. Diaphragm shortens and becomes flatter.

2. Intercostal muscles shorten, reducing the gaps between the ribs and making the ribs and sternum swing up and out.

3. Lungs are stretched larger, and air is sucked in.

Expiration

1. Diaphragm lengthens and resumes its dome shape.

2. Intercostals lengthen and allow the ribs and sternum to fall down and in.

3. Lungs return to smaller size and air is pushed out of them.

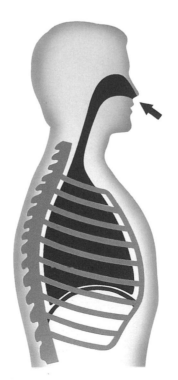

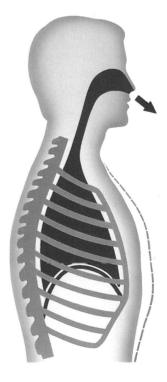

◀ **Normal expiration, or breathing out, is not powered by muscles. But if you want to blow up a balloon or do a similar blowing action, you use forced expiration. This involves muscles in the outer wall of the abdomen. They contract and squeeze the stomach and other contents of the abdomen. These press upward on the bases of the lungs and force the lungs to get smaller, so air is blown out hard.**

The actions of these breathing or respiratory muscles are shown in the diagrams. Together they enlarge the chest cavity and make the lungs bigger. As the lungs increase in volume, the air already in them becomes "stretched," which means its air pressure goes down. Outside the body, air pressure is slightly higher —it is normal atmospheric pressure. So some air moves from the region of higher pressure to lower pressure, that is, it flows into the lungs. In effect, air is sucked through the nose and throat, down the windpipe, and into the lungs.

Breathing out is a result of the lungs' elastic nature. When you stretch an elastic band, and let it go, it springs back to its normal smaller size. The lungs behave in the same way. The breathing muscles stretch the lungs bigger than their normal volume. Once these muscles relax and become floppy, the lungs spring back to their smaller size. This is called elastic recoil.

When people exercise, the muscles need extra oxygen and energy. To get the extra oxygen, breathing becomes faster and deeper. More muscles are used for deeper, harder breathing, including those in the shoulders, back, and abdomen. Rapid breathing continues after exercising to replace oxygen used during exercise.

FACT BOX

• An adult at rest breathes in and out about 12 to 16 times each minute. This is called the respiratory rate.

• A newborn at rest breathes in and out about 40 to 50 times each minute.

• A ten-year-old child at rest breathes in and out about 20 times each minute.

Gas Exchange

The muscle-powered movements of breathing continually suck fresh air into the lungs where some oxygen is absorbed from it and carbon dioxide is added to it. This process is called gas exchange. The stale air in the lungs is then blown out, and fresh air is sucked in again, and so on.

The more surface area that is available for gas exchange, the more efficient breathing becomes. The millions of alveoli in each lung provide a huge surface area. If all the alveoli were flattened out, they could cover an area of more than 750 sq. ft. (70 sq. meters)—20 or 30 times more than all of the skin over the body. Yet this huge surface is so curved and folded into the alveolar design that it fits neatly inside the lungs.

There is also a very thin barrier between the air in the alveoli and the blood in the capillaries around the alveoli (see the diagram on the opposite page). Most of this barrier is the watery fluid inside the flat cells forming the walls of each alveolus and capillary. Oxygen has a very short and easy journey. Carbon dioxide has an equally easy journey in the opposite direction.

The air that we breathe in is the same as the air all around us. It has the normal mixture of gases, mainly nitrogen and oxygen. Inside the lungs, some of the oxygen is taken out of the air, and carbon dioxide is added. So breathed-out air contains less oxygen and more carbon dioxide. ▶

Normal air breathed into lungs

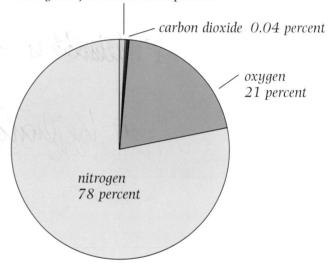

other gases just less than 1 percent

carbon dioxide 0.04 percent

oxygen 21 percent

nitrogen 78 percent

"Stale" air breathed out of lungs

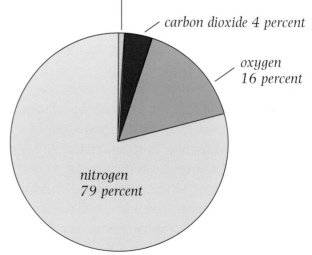

other gases just less than 1 percent

carbon dioxide 4 percent

oxygen 16 percent

nitrogen 79 percent

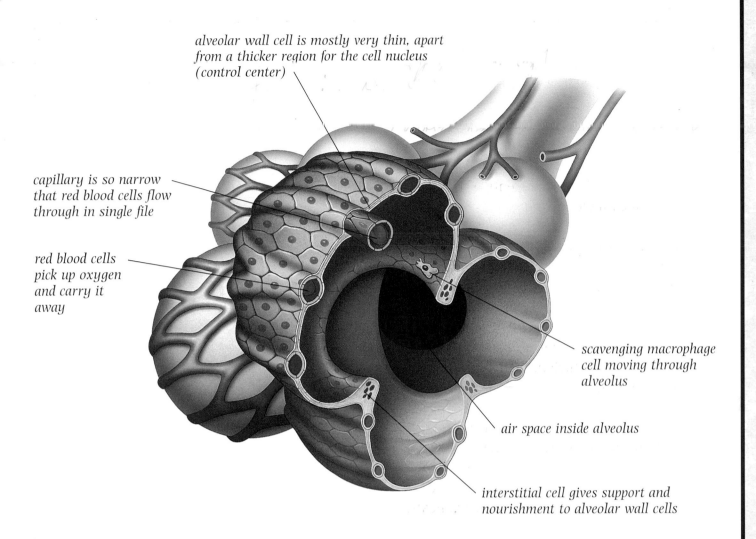

alveolar wall cell is mostly very thin, apart from a thicker region for the cell nucleus (control center)

capillary is so narrow that red blood cells flow through in single file

red blood cells pick up oxygen and carry it away

scavenging macrophage cell moving through alveolus

air space inside alveolus

interstitial cell gives support and nourishment to alveolar wall cells

▲ **In this extremely magnified view, the alveolus looks like a huge cave and the capillary like a giant tunnel. The walls of each are formed from flattened cells that have a curved shape, like bent stepping-stones.**

Why do these gases move at all? It is because of their concentrations or amounts. The blood flowing through the capillaries is very low in oxygen. The air in the alveoli has a much higher level or concentration of oxygen than this blood. So the oxygen naturally tries to spread itself out evenly and to make its concentration the same everywhere. This causes it to dissolve in the thin layer of fluid coating the inside of the alveolus and then pass in dissolved form, through the dividing cells into the blood. This movement of oxygen is called diffusion.

Most of the oxygen does not dissolve in the watery part of the blood. It is picked up and carried away by the doughnut-shaped red blood cells.

The reverse happens with carbon dioxide. Most of it is dissolved and combined with other chemicals in the watery part of the blood, rather than carried by red blood cells. Carbon dioxide is more concentrated in the blood than in the air inside the alveolus. So it diffuses from the blood, through the dividing cells, and out into the air inside the aveolus.

Blood Circulation

The respiratory system would be useless on its own. The body needs oxygen not only in the lungs, but in all of its parts. The task of spreading oxygen to all these cells is done by the circulatory system—the heart, blood vessels, and blood. So the respiratory system and circulatory system depend on each other to provide the body with oxygen and to keep it alive.

The heart pumps blood through the network of blood vessels. But the heart is not one pump. It is made up of two pumps, side by side, and there are also two networks of blood vessels. Blood from the heart's left-side pump flows out through arteries that take it all around the body. This blood releases its oxygen to the billions of cells. Then, low in oxygen and dark red in color, the blood flows back along veins to the heart's right-side pump.

The right pump forces out the deoxygenated blood along a different set of arteries—the pulmonary arteries, which lead to the lungs. These arteries branch many times, into the capillaries around each alveolus. Here the blood takes up new supplies of oxygen. As it does so, it changes color, becoming bright red. The capillaries join together to form the pulmonary veins. The refreshed, oxygenated, bright red blood flows back along the pulmonary veins to the heart's left-side pump, and the whole journey begins again.

We must not assume that all arteries contain bright red, oxygenated blood and that all veins contain dark red, deoxygenated blood. The pulmonary arteries contain dark red, deoxygenated blood, and the pulmonary veins convey bright red, oxygenated blood. An artery is simply a blood tube or vessel that carries blood away from the heart, and a vein is a vessel that returns it to the heart.

Blood circulation is continuous, with blood flowing in pulses through the vessels, pushed along by the pumping of the heart. On average, it takes a drop of blood about one minute to go around the body, back to the heart, around the lungs, and back to the heart again.

A baby in its mother's womb floats in a pool of fluid. It cannot breathe air, so it has a different layout of blood vessels inside its body. Blood low in oxygen and high in carbon dioxide flows from the baby along the umbilical cord—the baby's "lifeline"—to the placenta in the wall of the womb. Inside the placenta, the baby's blood comes very close to the mother's blood. Oxygen passes, or diffuses, from the mother's blood to the baby's blood, and carbon dioxide goes in the opposite direction. So for an unborn baby, the placenta does the same job as the lungs. The baby's lungs receive very little blood. At birth, the baby begins to breathe air. Its blood circulation changes in just a few minutes to the normal adult layout.

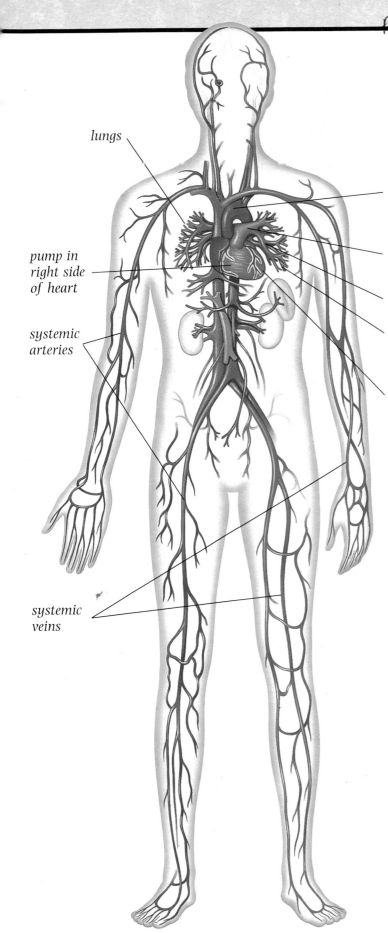

lungs

pump in
right side
of heart

systemic
arteries

systemic
veins

The body's circulation has two parts. One is
the pulmonary circulation, from the right side
of the heart through the lungs and back to
the left side of the heart. The other is the
systemic circulation, from the heart's left
side, around the rest of the body, and back to
the heart's right side.

*systemic circulation—the aorta
carries oxygenated blood away from
the heart to the rest of the body*

*the pulmonary artery carries
deoxygenated blood to the lungs*

pulmonary circulation

*the pulmonary veins carry
oxygenated blood from the lungs
back to the heart*

pump in left side of heart

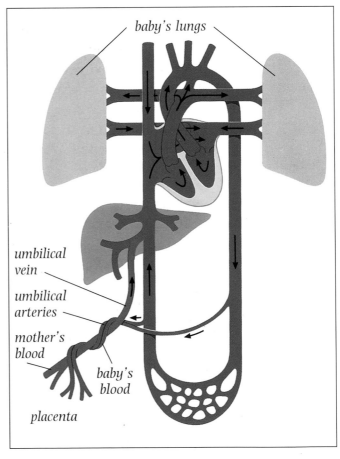

baby's lungs

umbilical
vein

umbilical
arteries

mother's
blood

baby's
blood

placenta

▲

The blood circulation of an unborn baby

Control of Breathing

Breathing, like most important body processes, is controlled by the brain. However, you do not have to remember to take every breath. If you did, you would have hardly any time to think about other things. Breathing, like the heart's beating, is controlled by the "automatic" part of the brain. It happens without your thinking about it. The parts of the brain that control breathing are together called the respiratory center.

There are four main parts to the respiratory center. Two are in the medulla, the stalklike base of the brain, just above the place where the brain merges into the spinal cord. These are the inspiratory and expiratory areas.

The inspiratory area is active for about two seconds at a time. It sends nerve signals down main nerves through the neck to the chest, telling the breathing muscles to contract for breathing in. It also sends signals to the expiratory area to keep it inactive. Then the inspiratory area's activity fades, and the expiratory area takes over for two or three seconds. The expiratory center sends nerve signals down to the chest, ordering the breathing muscles to relax for breathing out. It also sends signals to the inspiratory area, to keep it inactive. But in turn, the expiratory area fades, and the inspiratory area takes over again. This seesaw system controls the regular movements of normal breathing.

The other two parts of the respiratory center are higher up in the brain, in the region known

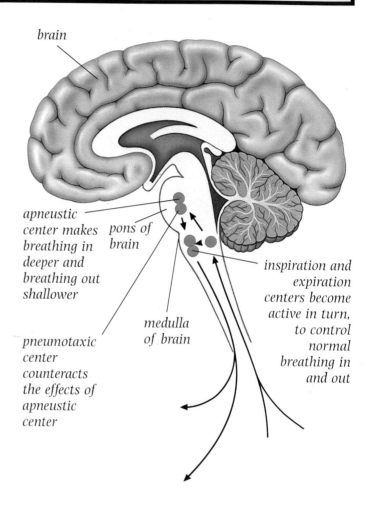

brain

apneustic center makes breathing in deeper and breathing out shallower

pons of brain

pneumotaxic center counteracts the effects of apneustic center

medulla of brain

inspiration and expiration centers become active in turn, to control normal breathing in and out

▲ The parts of the brain that control breathing are in its lower "automatic" region, where processes such as heartbeat, blood pressure, and digestion are also regulated.

as the pons. One is the apneustic area, which makes breathing in stronger but breathing out weaker. It becomes active when the body needs to breathe faster and harder and take in more oxygen during and after exercise. The other is the pneumotaxic area, which stops this change and returns breathing to normal.

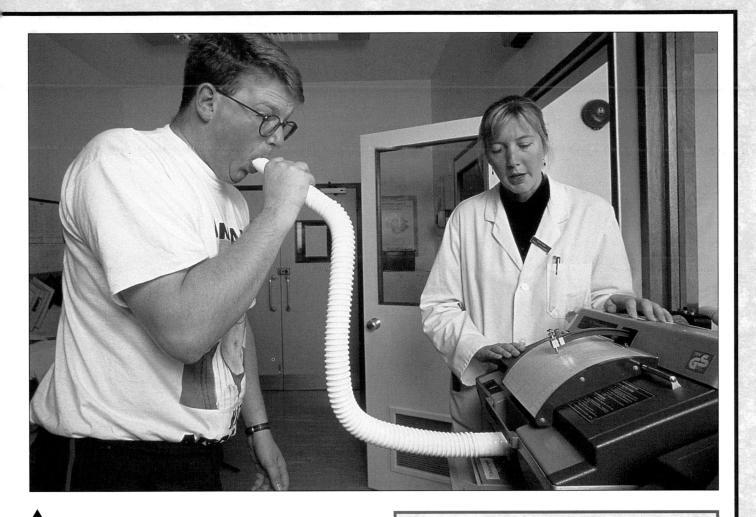

▲
A spirometer measures amounts of air breathed in and out of the lungs. It traces a pattern on a moving strip of paper or a TV screen, showing how much air is being breathed and how fast. A spirometer can help doctors to identify breathing problems or lung diseases.

There are several methods of controlling the respiratory center. Extra carbon dioxide in the blood makes it more acid. Sensors in the brain and main arteries detect this and tell the respiratory center. The respiratory center then speeds up breathing to get rid of the extra carbon dioxide. Sensors also detect the amount of oxygen in the blood, and, if this falls, they speed up breathing. During exercise, stretch sensors in muscles and joints detect lots of body movement, and they, too, speed up breathing.

FACT BOX

• At rest, an adult takes in and then gives out about 17 oz. (0.5 l) of air with each breath. This is the tidal volume.

• Breathing in as deeply as possible from normal takes in about 4 qts. (3.8 l) of air.

• Breathing out as deeply as possible from normal expels about 1 qt. (1 l) of air.

• The maximum amount that a man can breathe in and then out is 5 qts. (4.8 l). This is called the vital capacity of the lungs.

Respiratory Noises

Coughs

A cough is a sudden and noisy exhalation. Air is blasted up from the lungs and lower airways and out through the mouth. We usually cough to get rid of excess mucus or small bits of dust that have found their way down into the lower airways. First, there is a long in-breath, or inhalation. Then, muscles in the pharynx and larynx close them so air cannot escape. Next the muscles in the abdomen below the chest become tight and tense. This presses the intestines and other abdominal contents up against the chest, which makes the air pressure rise inside the chest. The pharynx and larynx open, and air rushes out at more than 60 mph (97 kph). It rattles the vocal cords as it blasts past them and pushes any loose mucus up into the pharynx, where it can be swallowed.

Sneezes

A sneeze is like a cough—a sudden and noisy exhalation. But the air comes out through the nose rather than the mouth, at 100 mph (160 kph), faster than the winds of a hurricane. We usually sneeze to get rid of excess mucus or small bits of dust in the upper airways, inside the nose. The first part of a sneeze is the same as for coughing. But the back of the tongue helps to block the airway while the abdominal muscles raise the air pressure in the chest. The air does not rattle the vocal cords as it rushes past them, and it blasts out through the nasal cavity, carrying a fine mist of loose mucus. This mist may spray 10 ft. (3 m). It carries germs that happen to be inside the nose, which other people may breathe in. For this reason, we should always sneeze into a disposable tissue or handkerchief.

◄ **A cough clears the lower airways of dust, excess mucus, smoke, irritating or harmful gases, and other unwanted substances.**

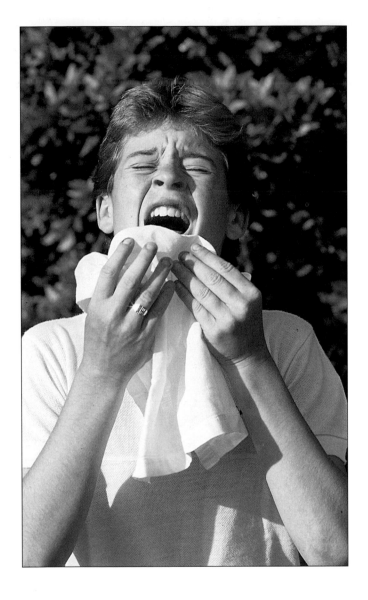

◄ **A sneeze squirts a fine spray or aerosol of nasal mucus out into the air. Pressing the bridge of the nose or the middle upper lip can help to delay it.**

yawn may force the muscles of the face into action. This draws more blood up into the head and brain and makes you feel less drowsy and more alert.

Hiccups (Hiccoughs)

Hiccups are short in-breaths that cannot be controlled. They are called "involuntary." They result from short contractions of the diaphragm muscle, which disturb regular contractions of normal breathing. The short contraction sucks in air quickly and makes the epiglottis at the top of the larynx snap shut with the "hick" noise. Some hiccups are due to a very full stomach, which presses on the diaphragm and nerves above and irritates them. Other hiccups have no clear cause.

Yawns

No one is quite sure why people yawn. They do it for a variety of reasons, such as when tired, inactive, bored, or excited. One possibility is that when the body stays still and quiet, breathing may not be fast or deep enough to get rid of carbon dioxide from the blood. This triggers a yawn, which is an extra-deep breath. It blows away the carbon dioxide from the blood out through the lungs and airways. Another possibility is that lack of oxygen triggers a yawn, for the same reason. Or the

Snoring

The sound of a snore is caused by air moving through the nose and pharynx and rattling the flexible rear roof of the mouth (the soft palate) and the uvula (the flap that hangs down at the upper back of the mouth). The sound may happen during inspiration or expiration. Snoring is most common in men 20 to 50 years old who are overweight and sleep on their backs, though anyone can snore. Cures include lying on one side or propping up the head with extra pillows.

Risks to the Respiratory System

The respiratory system is at risk from many dangers. The air going in and out may carry dirt, dust, germs, poisonous fumes, and other harmful substances. The sensitive lining of the airways can easily be damaged by vapors and chemicals. The very delicate alveoli are thin-walled so that they can absorb oxygen, but this also makes them vulnerable to damage.

The greatest threat is also the most preventable—smoking tobacco. The ingredients in tobacco smoke harm the lungs and many other parts of the body. The three chief ingredients are tars, carbon monoxide, and nicotine.

Tars irritate the airways, causing infections, such as bronchitis. They kill the cilia hairs, which no longer clean the lungs effectively. Mucus collects, produces a "smoker's cough" and increases risks of infection. Carbon monoxide causes narrowing of the arteries, so less oxygen can be carried in the bloodstream, and breathlessness results. Nicotine may raise blood pressure and clog blood vessels. Smokers are at greater risk of

- Heart attacks, raised blood pressure, and hardened arteries;

- Cancers in the mouth, throat, and lungs;

- Bronchitis, pneumonia, and other respiratory **infections**;

- Cancers of the esophagus, digestive system, bladder, and other body parts.

Secondary or passive smoking happens when someone breathes in tobacco smoke from other people. This also causes problems and illnesses. Children whose parents smoke are more likely to suffer from respiratory illnesses, such as colds and bronchitis, because they breathe in tobacco smoke at home.

Air pollution also increases the risk of respiratory conditions such as bronchitis and asthma. The air in a crowded city may be thick with fumes, smoke, and particles from vehicles, factory chimneys, power plants, and heating systems in houses and offices. The human respiratory system evolved in the clean air of the prehistoric world. It was never designed to cope with air pollution.

A person's job may increase the risk of respiratory problems. These include diseases such as miner's lung and farmer's lung. In many countries today, laws require that workers who are at risk from respiratory problems wear protective masks or that the workplace be supplied with clean, filtered air. However, these laws are sometimes ignored. ▶

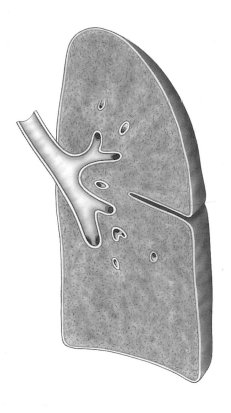

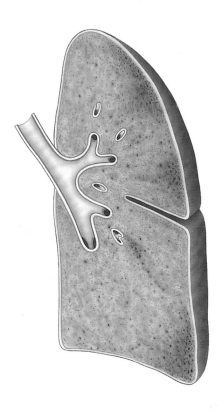

◄ The lungs of a baby are bright pink and clean. The lungs of an older person gradually become more gray and speckled with normal breathed-in particles of dust and dirt. But the lungs of a smoker (not shown) are blackened and clogged with tars and chemicals from tobacco smoke.

FACT BOX

What is in tobacco smoke?

- **Tars**—These turn to vapor in the smoke, then condense back into thick, sticky tars in the respiratory system.

- **Carbon monoxide**—This gas makes red blood cells less able to carry oxygen around the body.

- **Nicotine**—An addictive drug that has many harmful effects on the brain and nervous system.

Respiratory Infections

The air around us may look clean, but there are always microbes floating in it. Some of these are harmful to us and are known as germs. If they get into the body, they multiply and cause the types of illness called infections. The respiratory system is especially at risk from infections. The air passing through it is almost certain to carry germs at some time. These can enter the delicate linings of the airways and alveoli and get into the body easily. When the affected person coughs or sneezes, mucus and germs are sprayed into the air and may be breathed in by someone else.

A cough is not a disease or illness in itself. It is a symptom caused by an underlying disease or illness such as pharyngitis or bronchitis. The cough is simply an action to clear the lower airways. The common cold is a disease or rather, lots of similar diseases, caused by infection with viruses. Cold symptoms include sneezing and a nose that is sore, itchy and stuffy, or runny. There are about 200 different viruses that cause colds. Although the body may catch and defeat one type, this does not give protection against the others. That is why the "common cold" stays so common.

Infection in each part of the respiratory system has its own name, usually the name of the body part with "-itis" on the end. The "-itis" ending means inflammation, which is swelling, soreness, and redness. The condition may be due to infection by germs or to another problem, such as an allergy. ▶

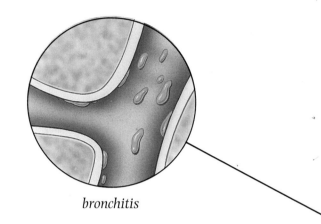

bronchitis

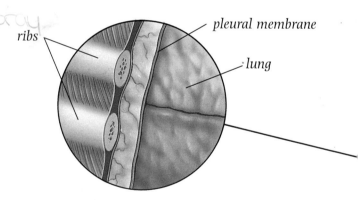

ribs *pleural membrane* *lung*

pleurisy

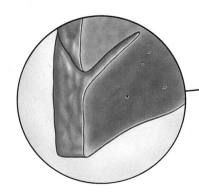

pneumonia

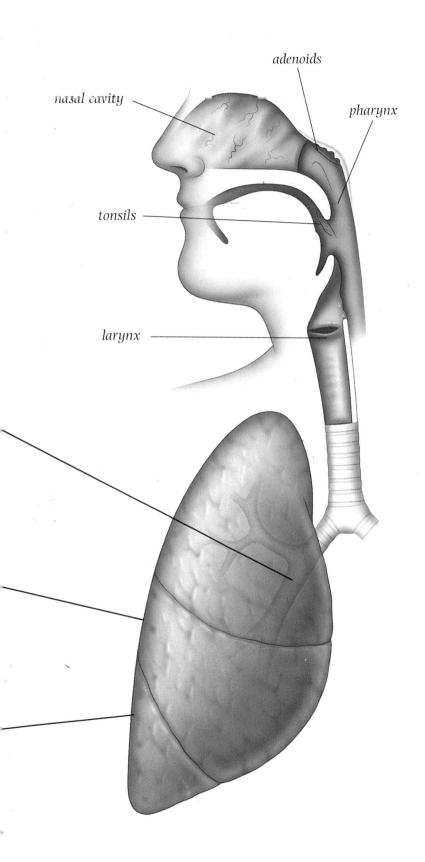

nasal cavity

adenoids

pharynx

tonsils

larynx

The common cold is an infection of the linings in the nasal cavity and other parts of the airway system. It can cause a runny or blocked nose, watering eyes, sneezing, sore throat, and headache.

A sore throat may be pharyngitis, laryngitis, or even tonsillitis. The symptoms are pain, soreness, and swelling in the throat and neck, coughing, a fever (raised body temperature), hoarseness, and pain when swallowing.

Influenza begins with an infection in the nose or throat and spreads to affect many body parts. It causes chills or fever, headache, sneezing, sore throat, coughing, and aches and pains in the muscles and joints.

Bronchitis affects the main air tubes, or bronchi, in the lungs. The linings of the bronchi become swollen, narrowing the space inside for air to pass through. They also produce extra mucus. The symptoms are coughing, breathlessness, wheezing, and fever.

Pleurisy is swelling and soreness of the pleural membranes around each lung. It makes breathing difficult and painful. It is often a complication of another disease, such as pneumonia.

Pneumonia is inflammation of the lung tissues. It causes a variety of symptoms such as a cough, fever, breathlessness, chills and sweats, and chest pains. There are many causes, from infection by germs to the inhaling of poisonous fumes.

Respiratory Conditions

Some respiratory conditions do not involve germs. The most common of these are due to **allergies**. Most allergies involve the body's reacting against normally harmless substances, such as minute pollen grains floating in the air. The body's immune defense system attacks the harmless substances, as though they were invading harmful germs. Often this causes inflammation.

Different allergic reactions affect different parts of the body. In the respiratory tract, well-known examples are hay fever (also called seasonal rhinitis) and asthma. The cause of hay fever is usually microscopic pollen grains drifting in breathed-in air. Some people are allergic to grass pollen and others to pollen from certain flowers or particular trees. Hay fever comes on at the time of year when these plants produce most pollen. Perennial rhinitis is similar to hay fever, but it can occur at any time. It may be caused by dust, animal fur or feathers, or similar airborne particles.

A person suffering from asthma has episodes of breathlessness and wheezing and a tight feeling in the chest. In most cases, it is due to constriction, or tightening, of the muscles in the walls of the lower respiratory air tubes, the bronchi, and bronchioles. The muscle contraction narrows these tubes. Their linings may become inflamed and produce extra mucus, which makes the airways even narrower.

Asthma attacks usually fade naturally after a short time. Rarely does the affected person become so breathless that his/her life is in danger. The attacks can be treated with drugs. Bronchodilator drugs dilate, or widen, the airways by making their wall muscles relax. These drugs are breathed in as a fine spray from an inhaler device, so they quickly reach the bronchi and bronchioles.

Asthma usually develops during the first few years of life. In some people it fades with increasing age. It has also become more common in recent years. The "trigger factors" that start an episode vary from person to person. They include

- Particles or dust in the air, such as pollen grains, animal fur, or feathers;

- Tiny creatures called housemites, and their dried, powdery droppings drifting in the air;

- Certain foods, such as eggs and milk;

- Drugs;

- Exercise or exertion;

- Sudden exposure to cold or heat;

- Worry or shock;

- Infection, especially from the respiratory system.

Hay fever and other forms of rhinitis affect the lining of the nasal cavity. It becomes inflamed and makes excess mucus. This causes an itchy, runny nose and sneezing. The eyes and throat may also be itchy and red.

Laryngitis can happen without infection by germs. One cause is shouting too much or straining the voice in some way. It makes the larynx sore and painful and the voice hoarse and croaky.

Asthma affects the bronchi and bronchiole air tubes in the lungs. They become tightened, narrowed, and clogged with mucus, causing shortness of breath for a time.

Emphysema involves the air bubbles, or alveoli, in the lungs. They become stretched and stiff, and they may burst or merge together. This reduces the area for obtaining oxygen. The main symptom is shortness of breath. Emphysema may accompany long-term bronchitis or asthma and is more common among smokers.

There are many types of lung cancers, due to different causes. The type called bronchial carcinoma is nearly always found in people who smoke.

Pneumoconiosis is the name for a group of illnesses known as "dust diseases." They are the result of breathing in dust particles over many years, and they are usually linked to a person's job. They include coal-miner's lung, farmer's lung, silicosis, and asbestosis.

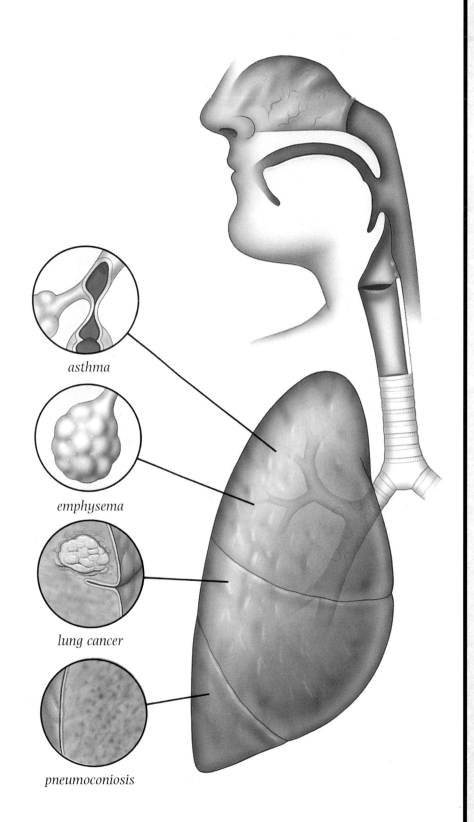

asthma

emphysema

lung cancer

pneumoconiosis

Respiratory Emergencies and First Aid

Oxygen is essential for life, and anything that interferes with breathing, or getting oxygen into the body, is very serious. If an object gets into the airways, especially the larynx or trachea, it can block the tube and keep air from going past. It causes choking. The body's natural reaction is to cough and to try and blow the object out again.

Another emergency is strangulation. This happens when a cord, tie, rope, or similar object is tied too tightly around the neck. It squashes the airway closed and stops fresh air from getting to the lungs. It is one reason that people should never tie or loop ropes or similar things around the neck, even in fun.

A drowning person breathes water, not air. There is oxygen dissolved in water, but unlike a fish's gills, our lungs are not designed to obtain it. In many cases the water does not get deep into the lungs. It blocks the main airways, such as the bronchi. Anyone who has almost drowned or breathed in water should receive medical attention. The respiratory system may

▼ **Part of cardiopulmonary resuscitation (CPR) is artificial ventilation or the "kiss of life." It involves breathing air into the casualty's lungs. This helps because breathed-out air contains oxygen. First-aiders are taught how to do this procedure correctly to avoid hazards, such as the risk of infection.**

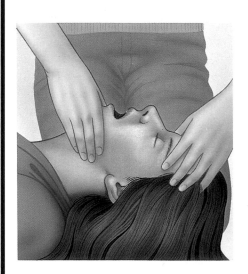  

1. *Instruct someone to call an ambulance. Check the mouth for any blockage and remove if possible. Lay the casualty on his or her back and tip the head back to straighten the main airways.*

2. *Hold the nose closed so air cannot escape through it. Seal lips over the casualty's mouth and blow air into the casualty's lungs, checking that the chest rises.*

3. *Let the chest fall as air escapes. Repeat the process until medical help arrives.*

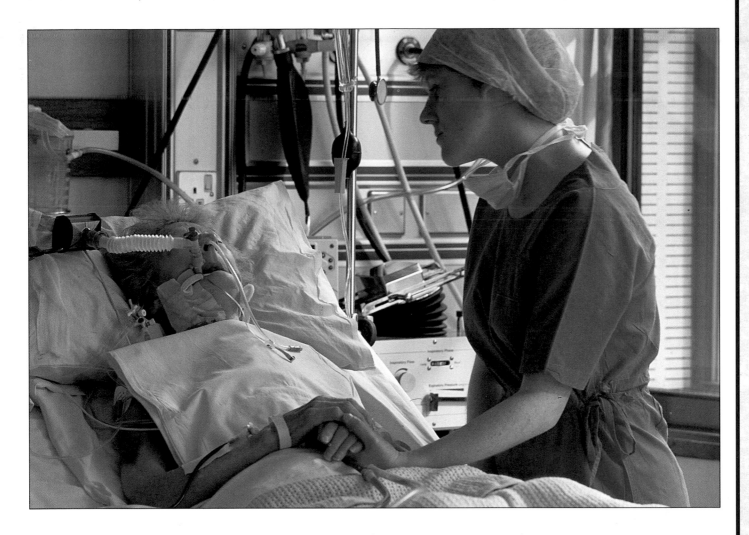

react later with soreness and inflammation, and there is also a greater risk of infection.

Suffocation is caused by a lack of oxygen. It can be the result of choking, strangulation, or drowning—or of breathing certain gases. Carbon monoxide is especially dangerous. Red blood cells attach to it much more easily than to oxygen, and they do not let it go. The blood soon becomes "full" of carbon monoxide, so it cannot supply oxygen to the body's cells. Carbon monoxide occurs in tobacco smoke and the exhaust fumes from cars and other vehicles.

The most serious emergency occurs when a person stops breathing for any reason. Doctors, nurses, ambulance crews, and qualified first-aiders are trained to get the breathing started again, and the heart, too, if it has stopped beating. This is called cardiopulmonary ("heart-lung") resuscitation (CPR).

▲ **The intensive care unit of a hospital is for extremely ill people. If they have trouble breathing, they can be helped by a mechanical ventilator. This machine pumps a special mixture of oxygen-rich gases through a tube, in and out of the lungs, to mimic the body's breathing movements.**

Glossary

Allergy A condition in which the body is sensitive to a normally harmless substance and reacts to it, often with inflammation (redness, soreness, and swelling)

Alveoli Microscopic air sacs at the end of a terminal bronchiole air tube in the lung

Arteries Large blood vessels that carry blood away from the heart

Arterioles Small blood vessels linking arteries and capillaries

Biochemical Describing chemical changes or reactions in living things

Bronchi The main air tubes in the lungs. They divide further to form bronchioles.

Bronchioles The smallest and thinnest air tubes in the lungs

Capillaries Very tiny blood vessels that link arterioles and venules

Cartilage Strong, pale body tissue that is softer and more flexible than bone

Cilia Microscopic hairs on the surface of some cells. Cilia wave back and forth, filtering and transporting dust particles and dirt.

Deoxygenated Low or lacking in oxygen

Diaphragm The curved sheet of muscle under the lungs that is involved in breathing

Gas exchange Gas exchange takes place in the lungs. Oxygen from the air is transferred to the blood and carbon dioxide from blood to the air.

Infection A condition in which germs get into the body, live, multiply, and cause illness

Intercostals Straplike muscles between the ribs, involved in breathing

Larynx The larynx, or voice box, sits in the neck, at the top of the windpipe, and makes the sounds of the human voice.

Microbes Living things that are so small they can only be seen through a microscope. If they are harmful, they are called germs.

Mucus Sticky substance that forms the natural protective lining to the nose, mouth, airways, and other body parts

Oxygenated High or plentiful in oxygen

Pharynx The pharynx, or throat, links the back of the nose and mouth to the top of the esophagus (gullet) and trachea (windpipe).

Respiration (1) Bodily respiration—the movements or process of breathing; (2) Cellular or aerobic respiration—the chemical changes inside a cell that use oxygen and release energy from food

Sinus A hole or cavity such as the air-filled nasal sinuses in the skull bone

Systemic circulation The route taken by the blood around the body, carrying vital oxygen, as opposed to the pulmonary circulation

Trachea The windpipe, linking the throat to the lungs in the chest

Veins Large blood vessels carrying blood to the heart

Venules Small blood vessels linking capillaries to veins

Books to Read

Bryan, Jenny. *Breathing: The Respiratory System*. Body Talk. Morristown, NJ: Silver Burdett Press, 1993.

Burnie, David. *The Concise Encyclopedia of the Human Body*. New York: Dorling Kindersley, 1995.

Catherall, Ed. *Exploring the Human Body*. Exploring Science. Austin, TX: Raintree Steck-Vaughn, 1992.

Silverstein, Alvin. *Respiratory System*. Human Body Systems. New York: 21st Century Books, 1994.

Ward, Brian. *Breathing: And Your Health*. Health Guides. Danbury, CT: Franklin Watts, 1991.

Index